Lacy Sunshine's
Bubbles Fairy Coloring Book Volume 13

Illustrated by Heather Valentin

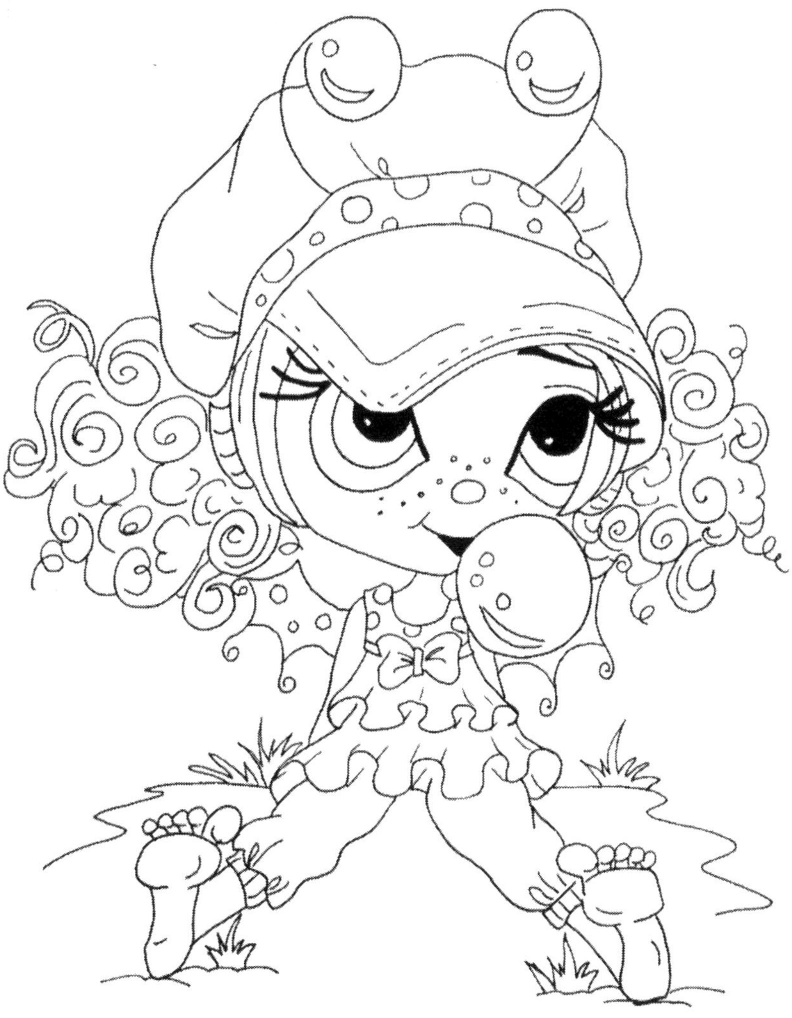

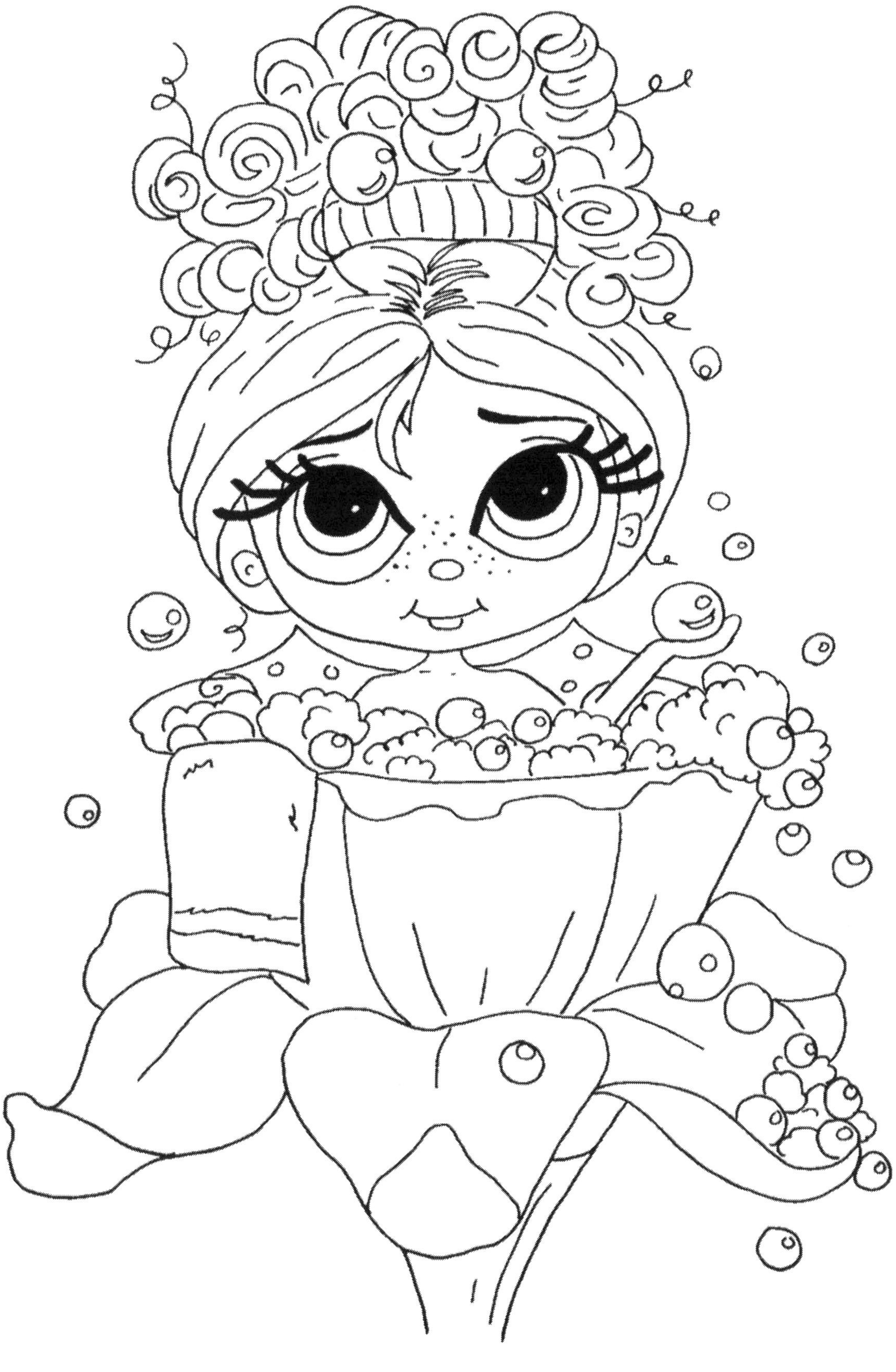

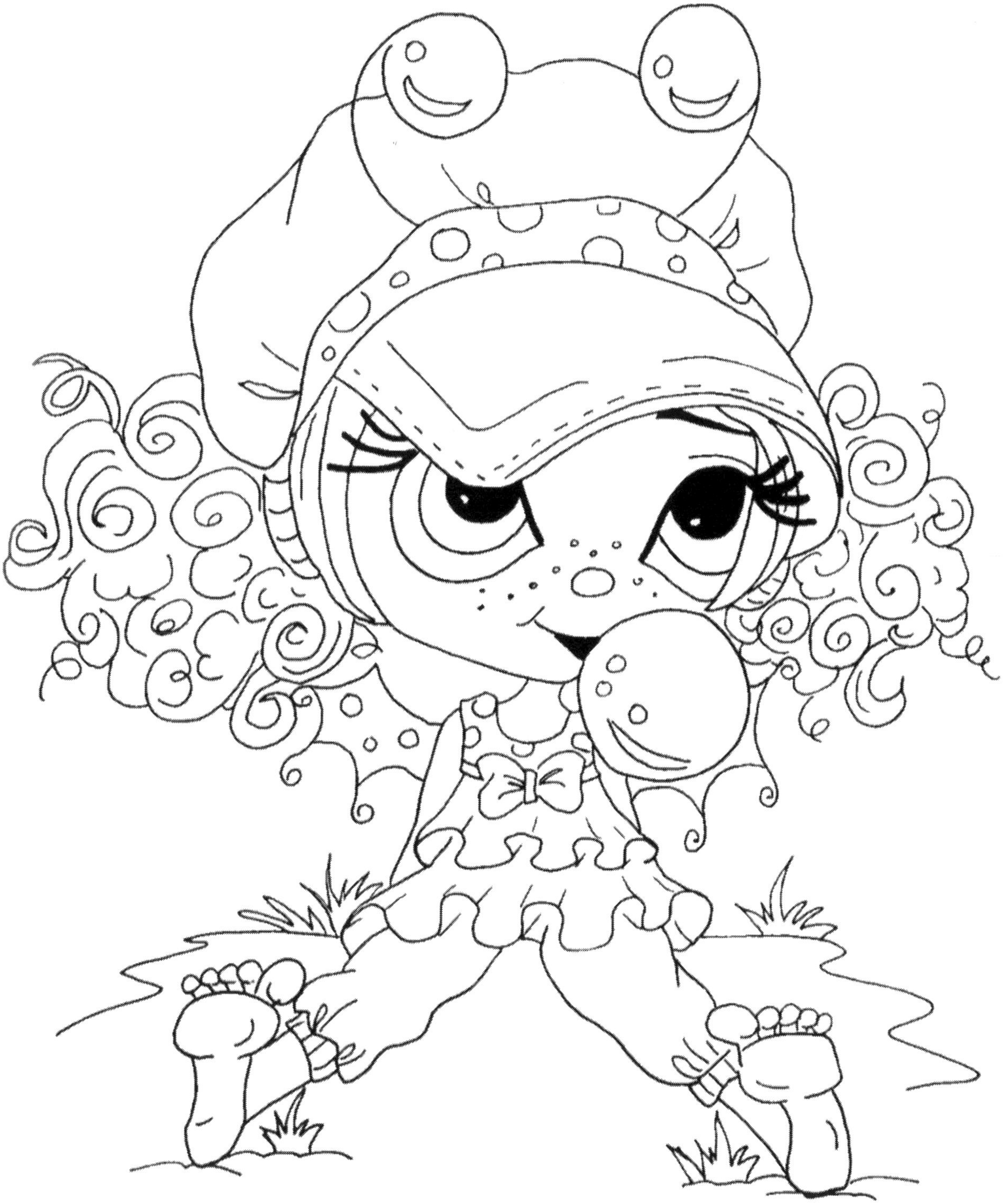

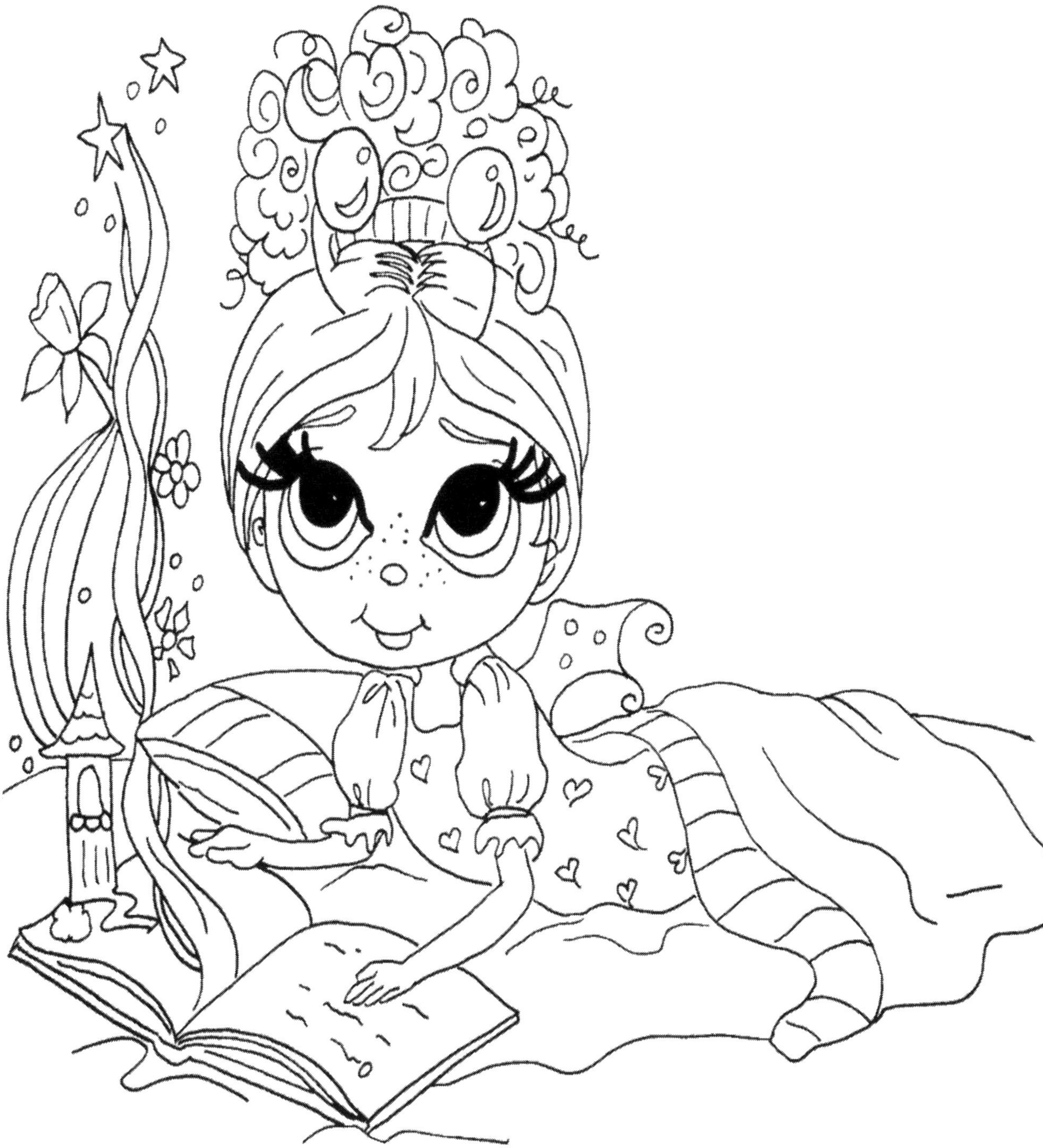

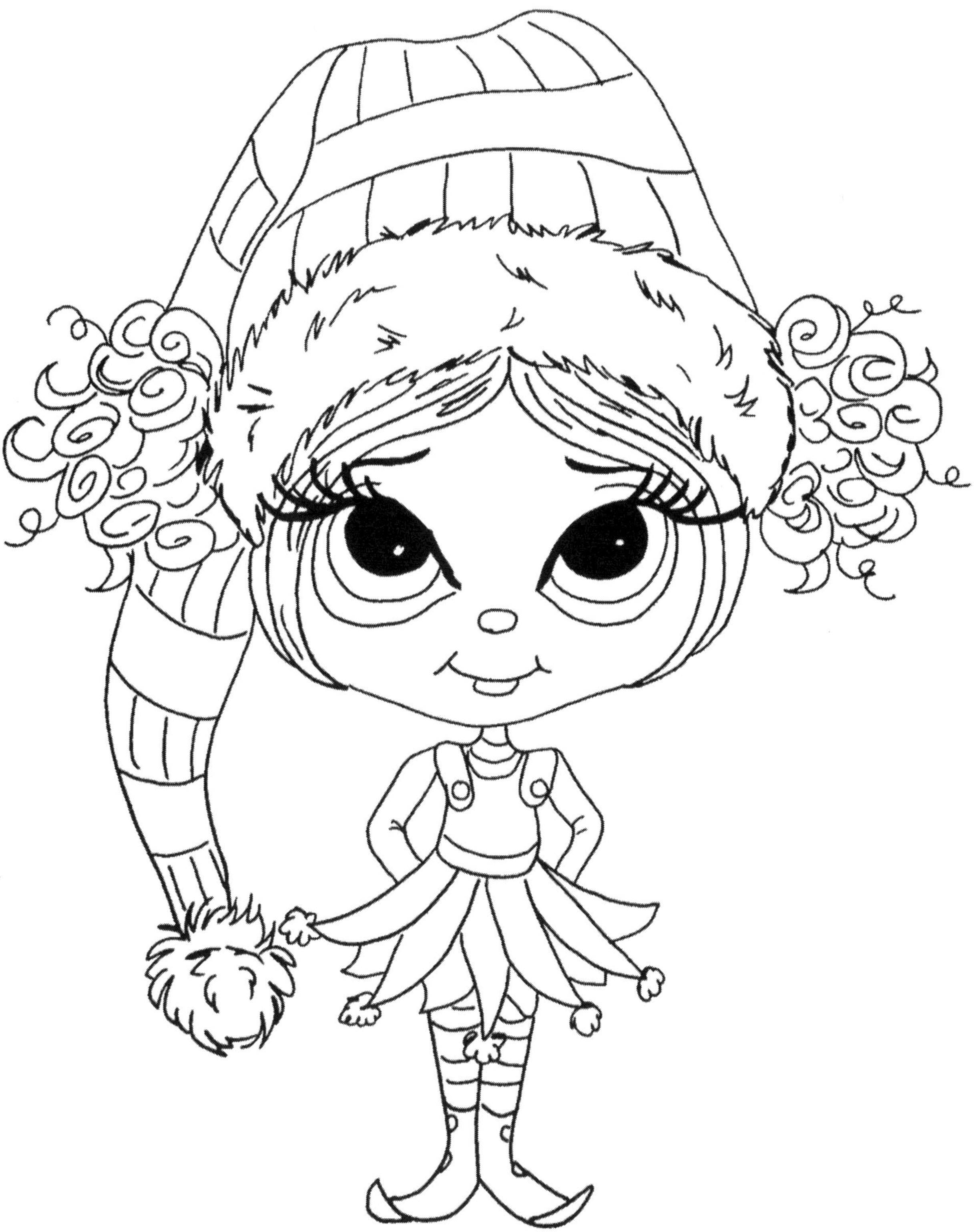

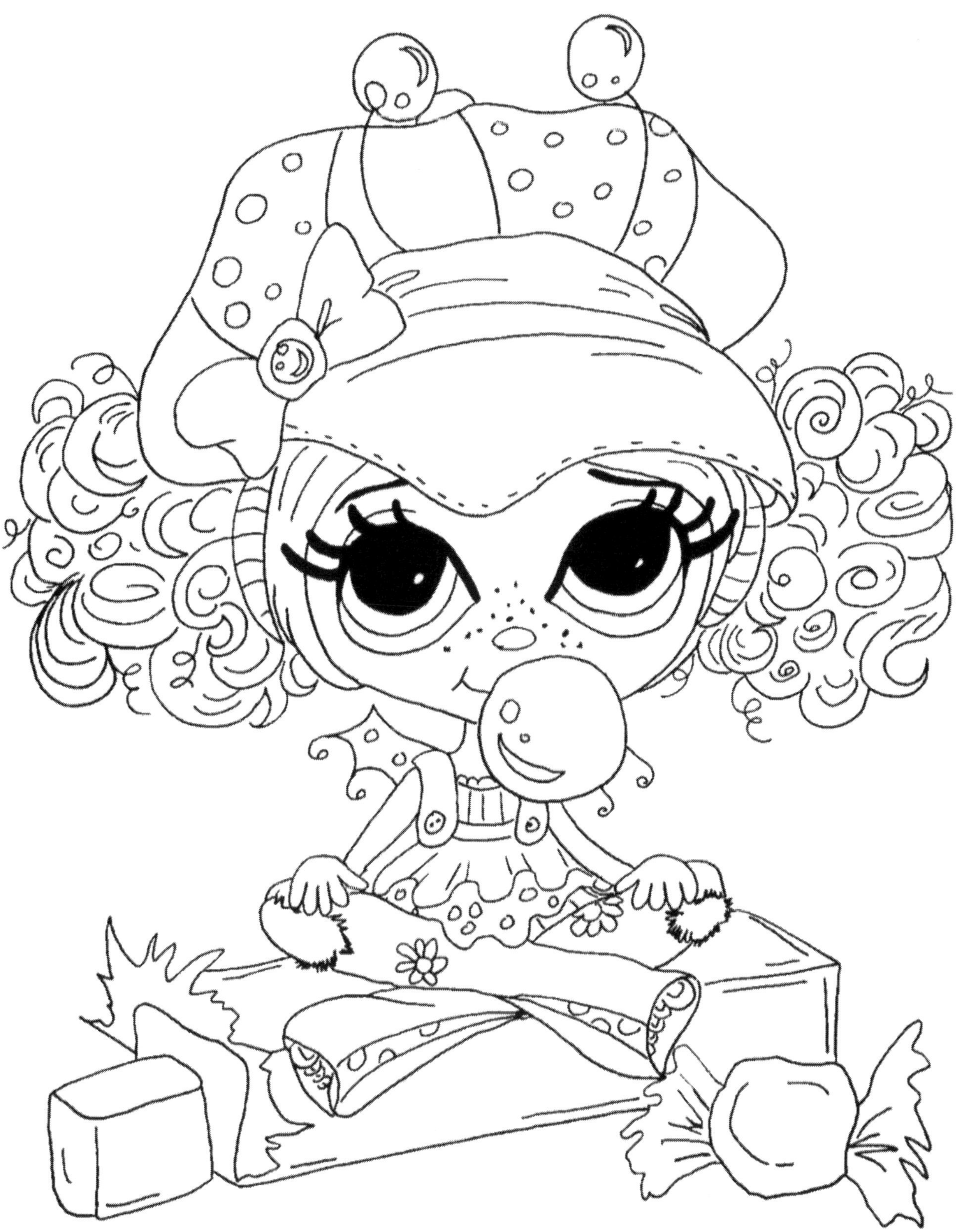

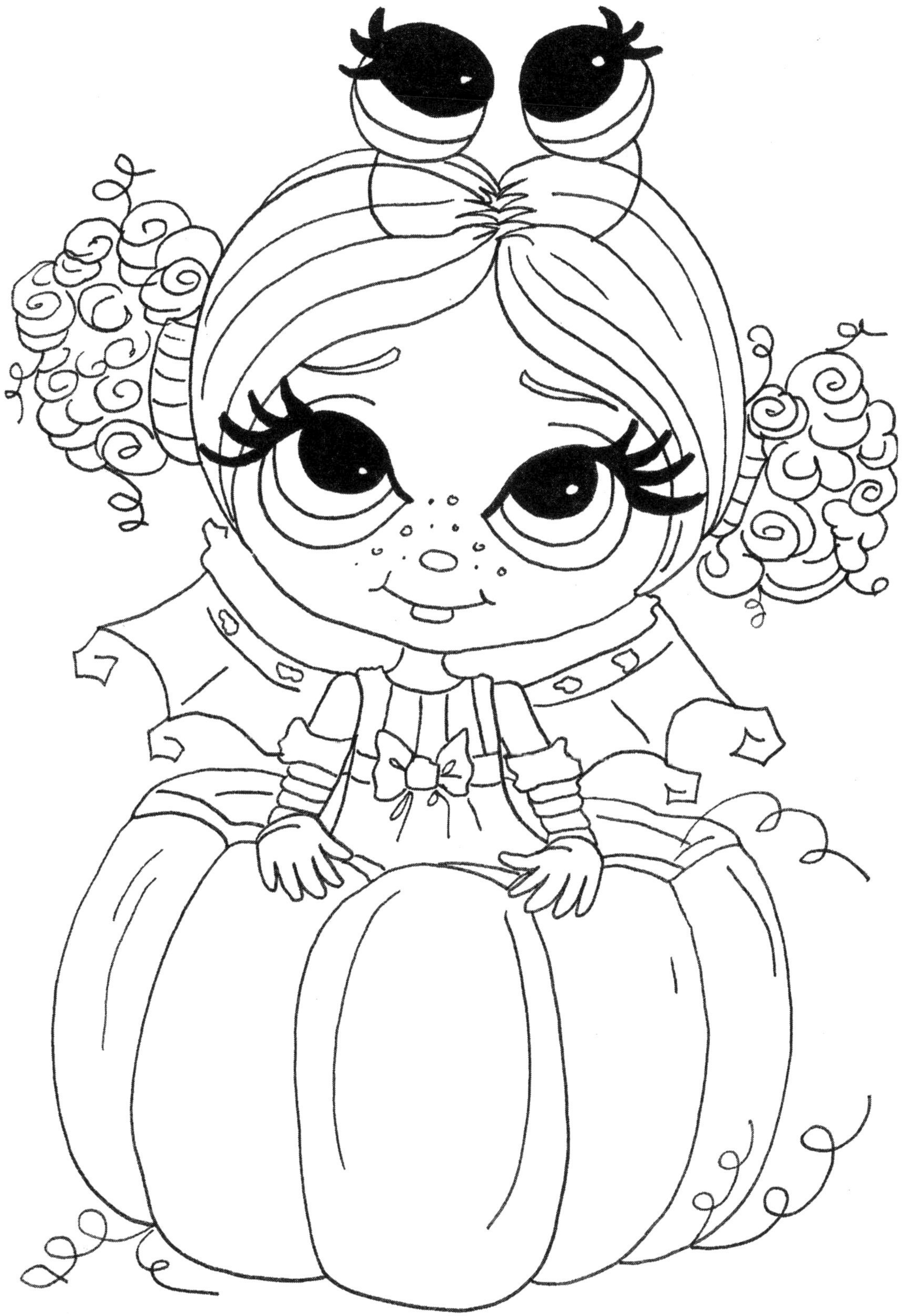

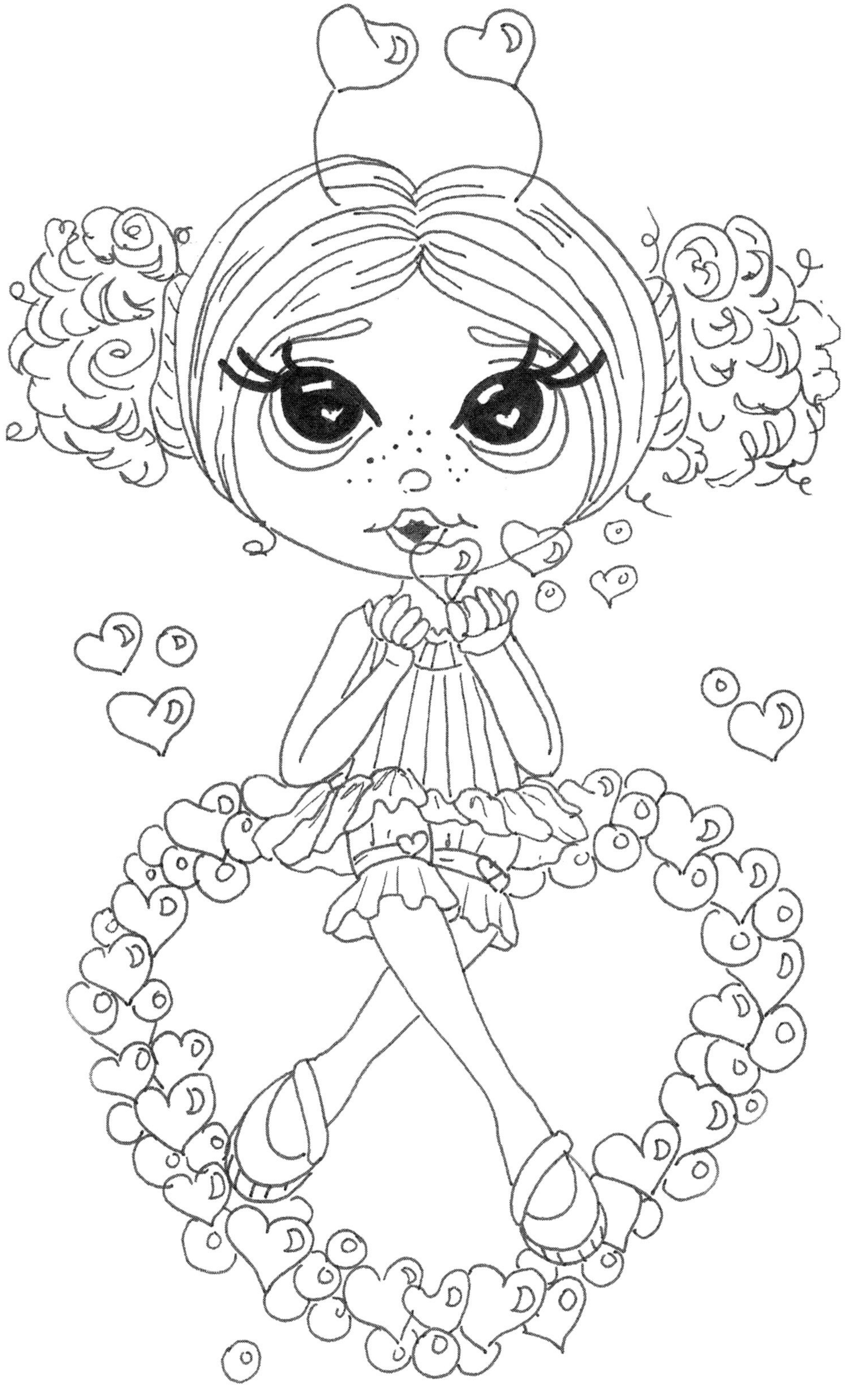

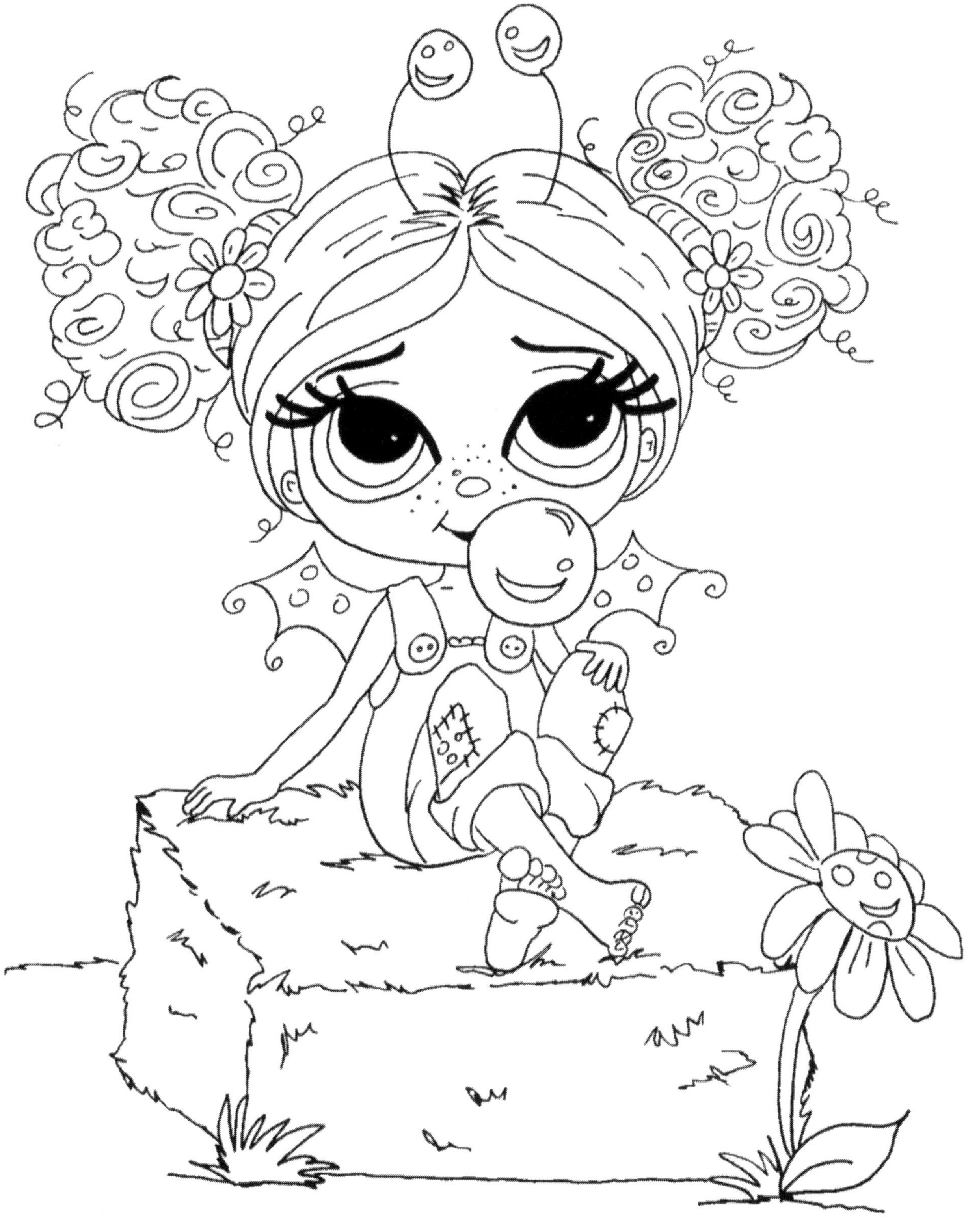

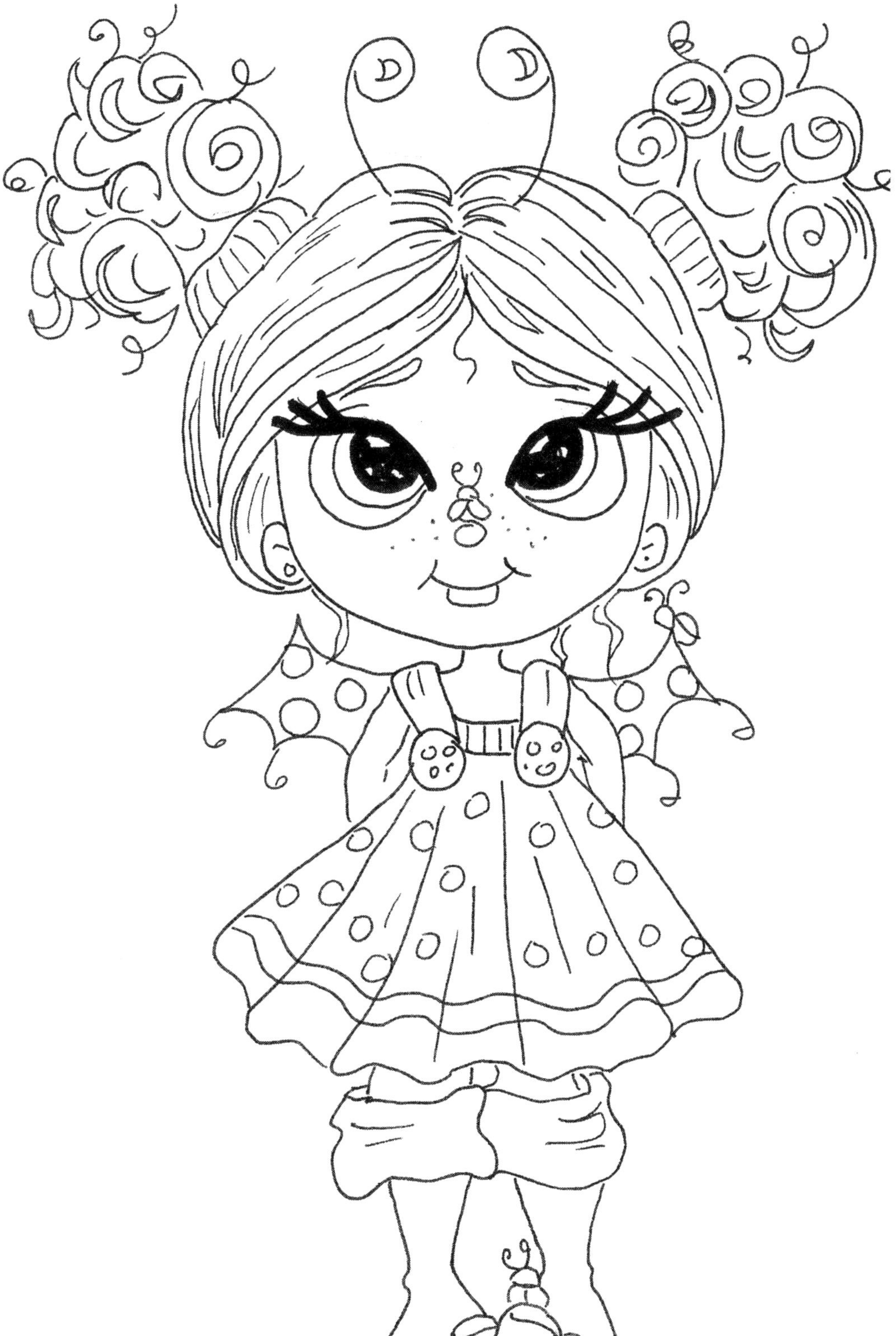

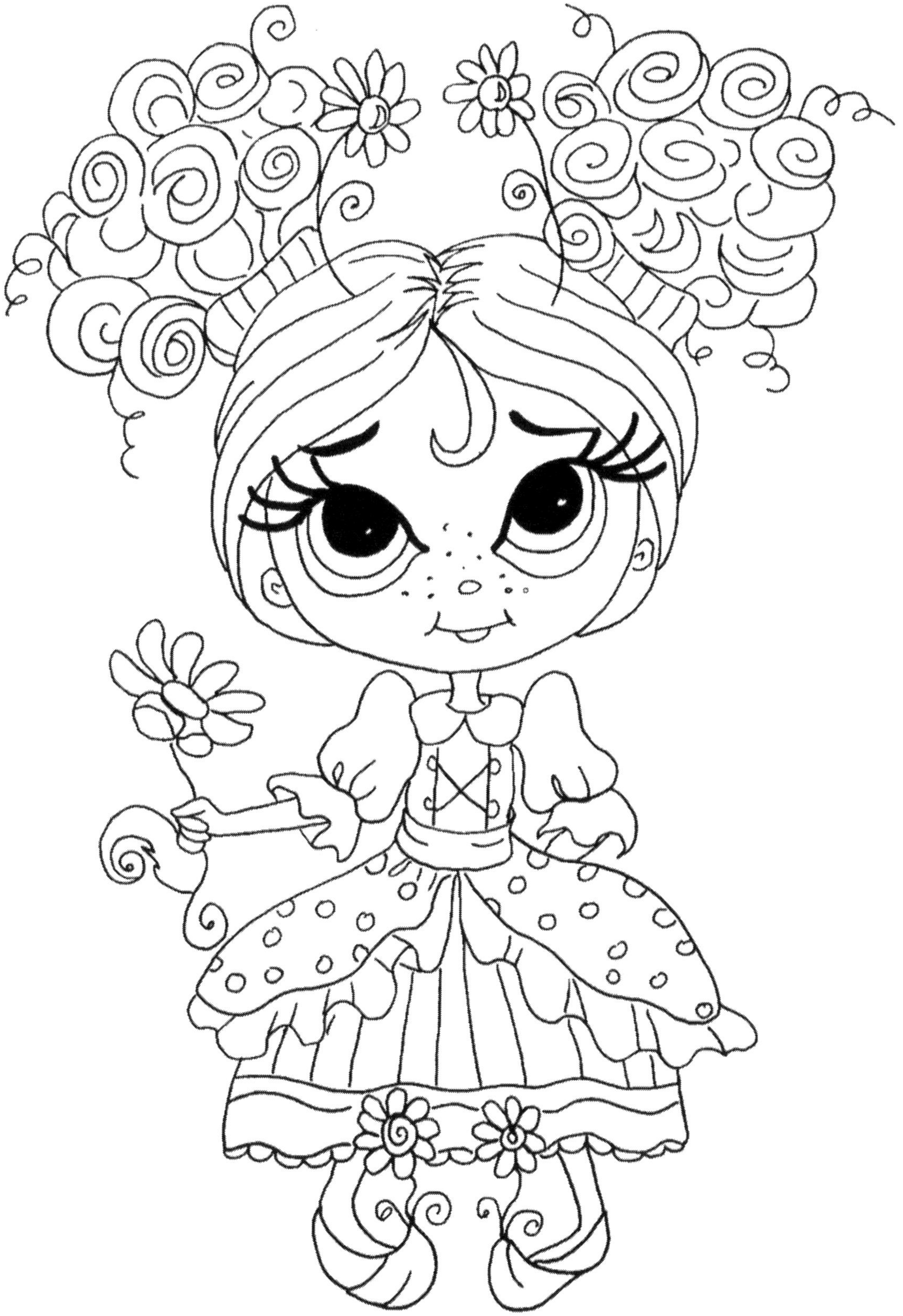

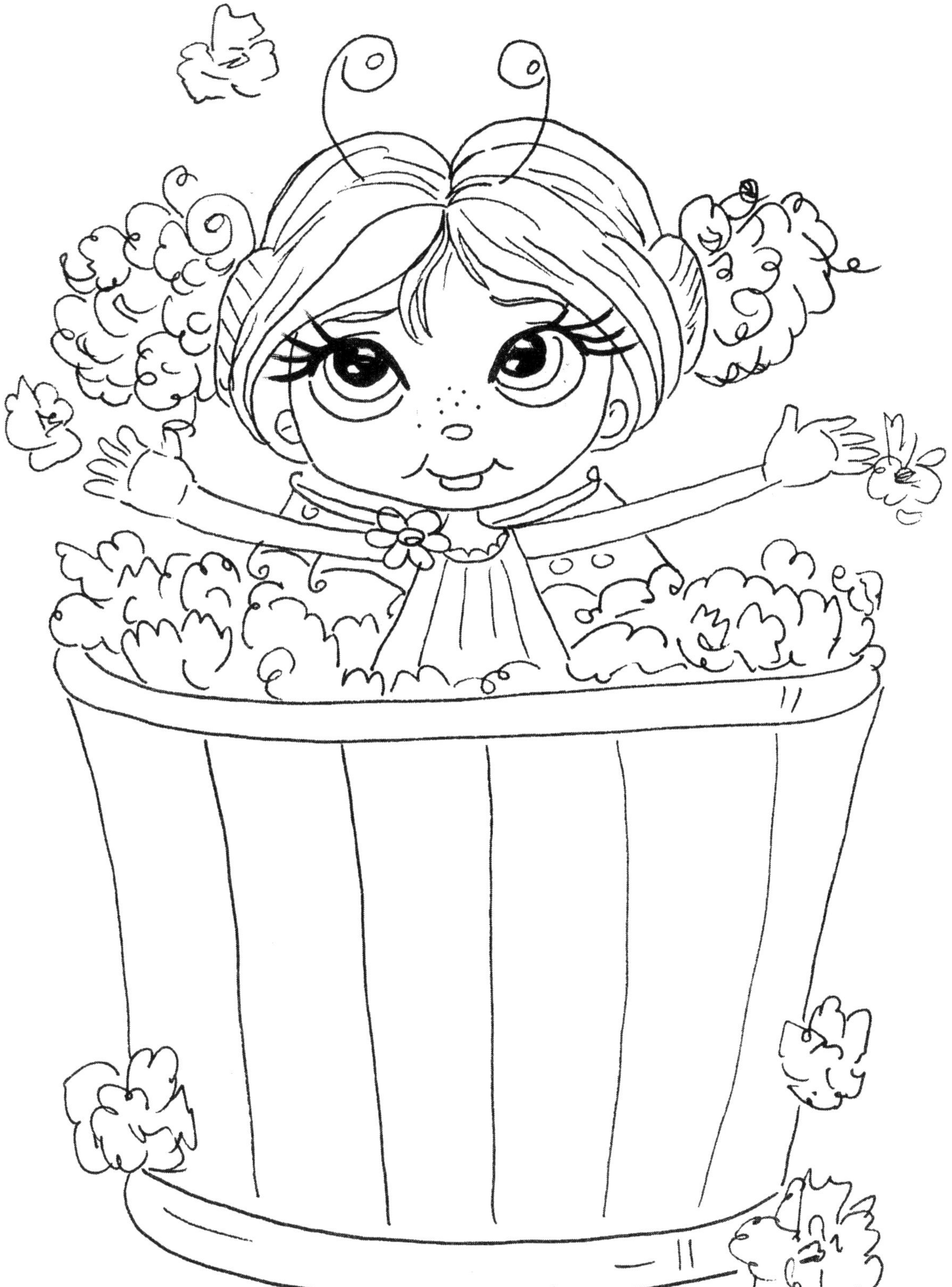

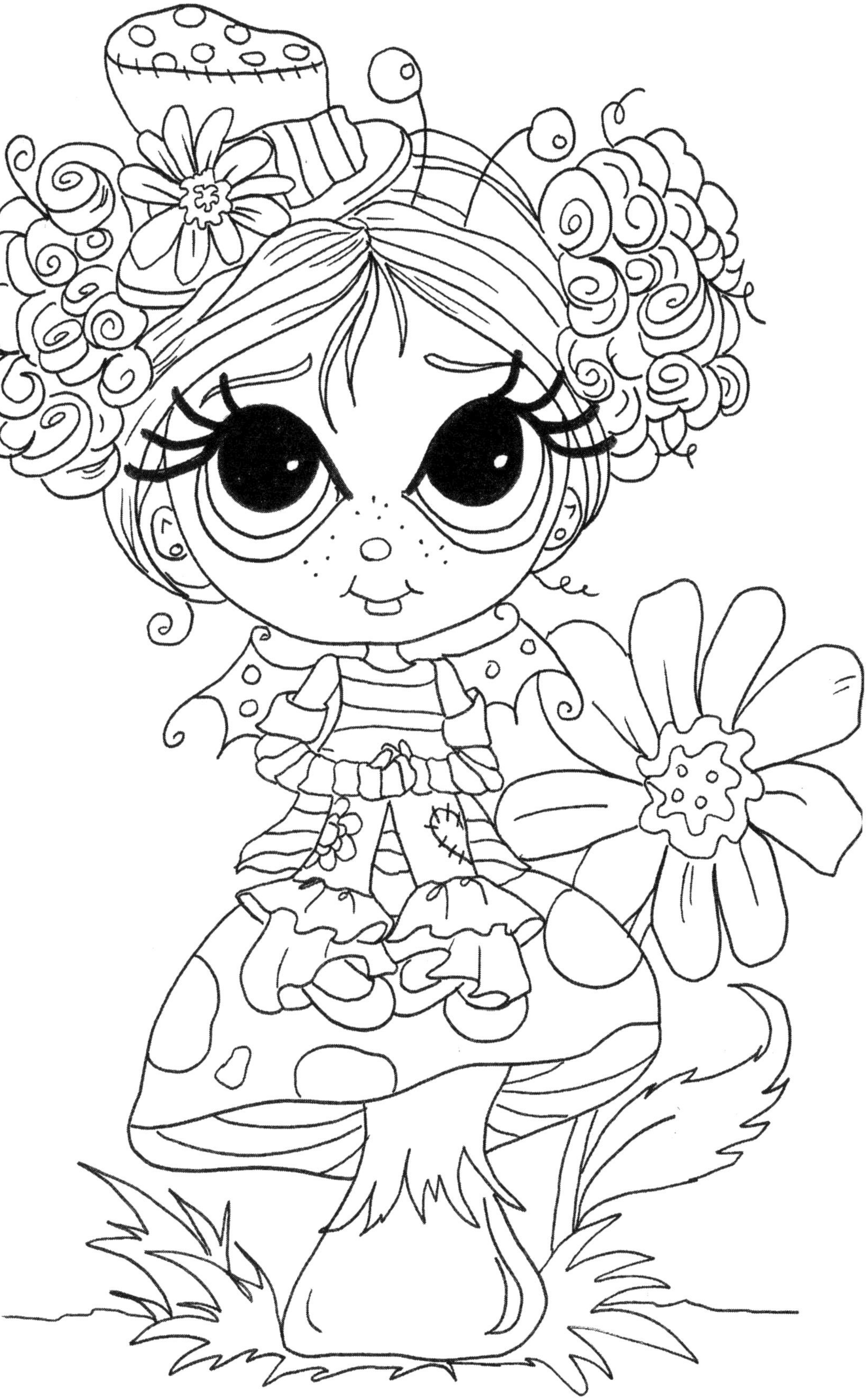

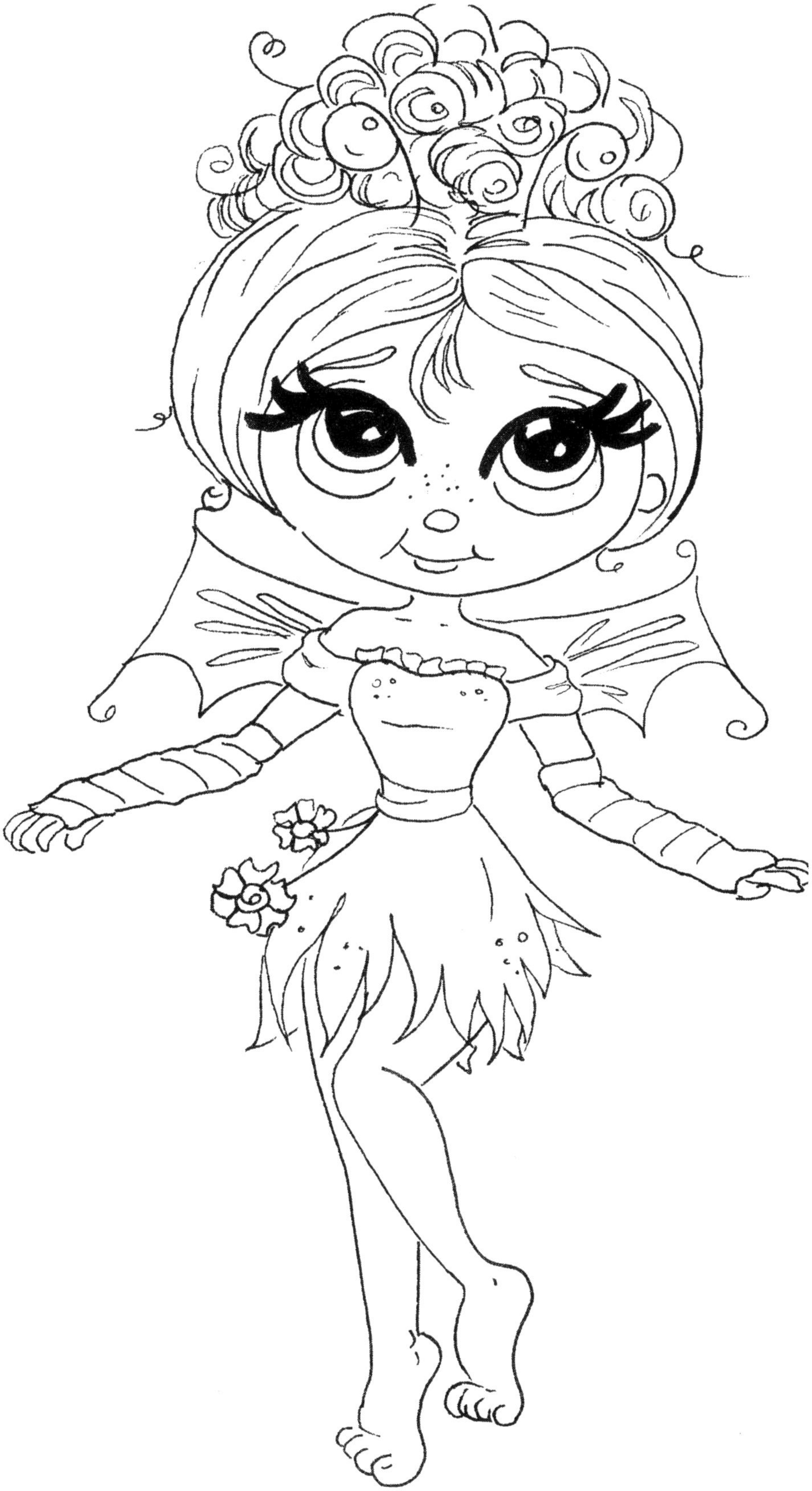

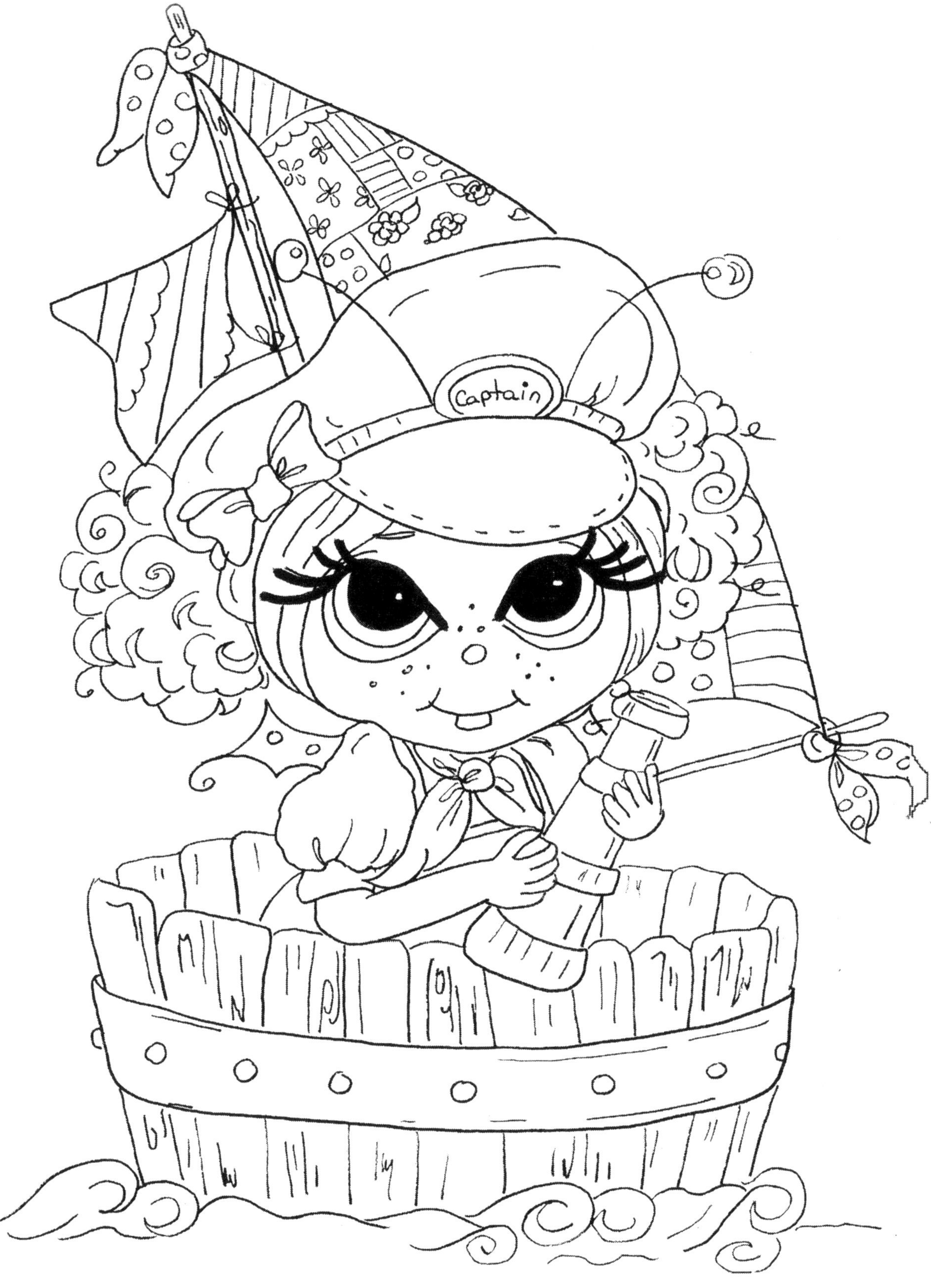
Captain

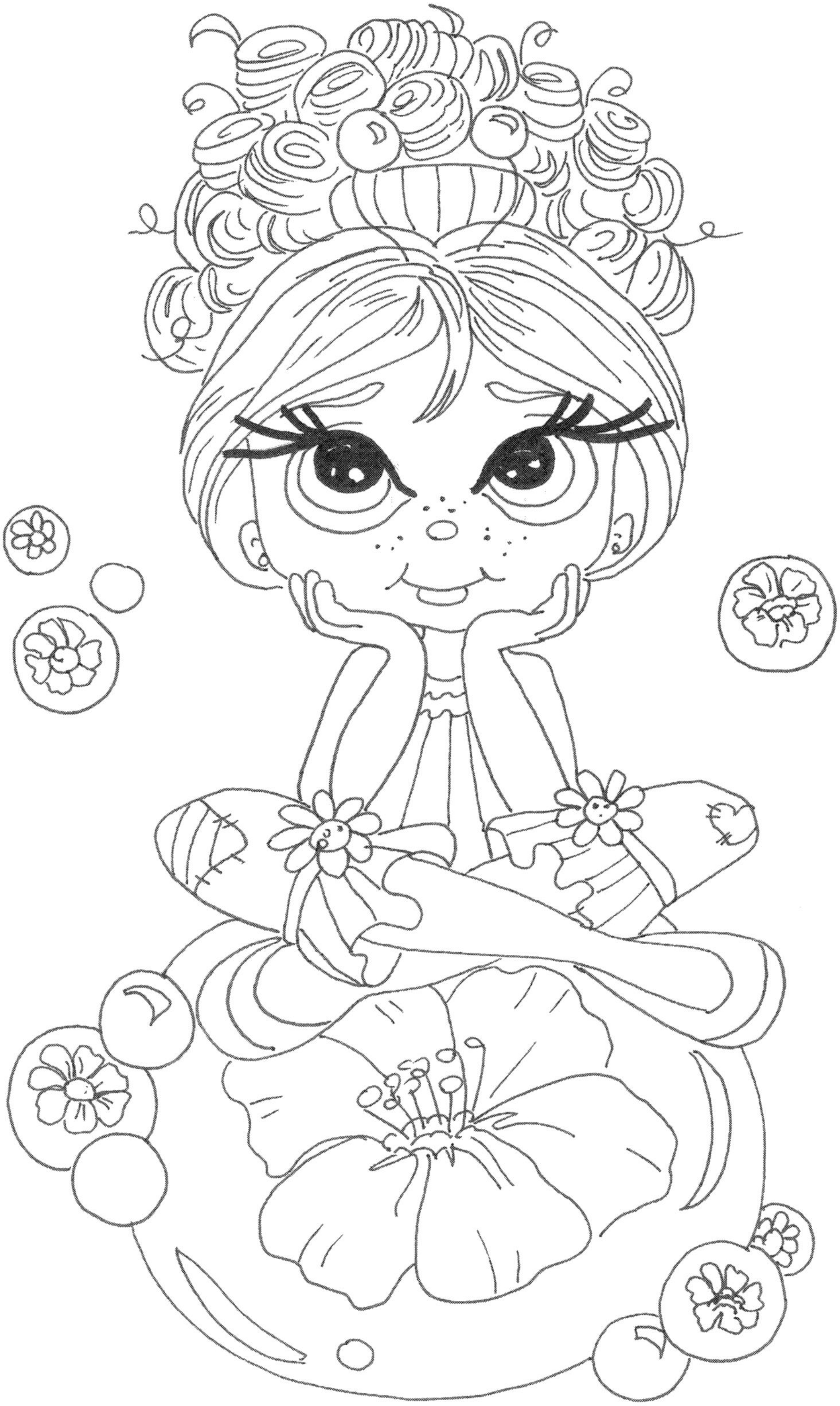

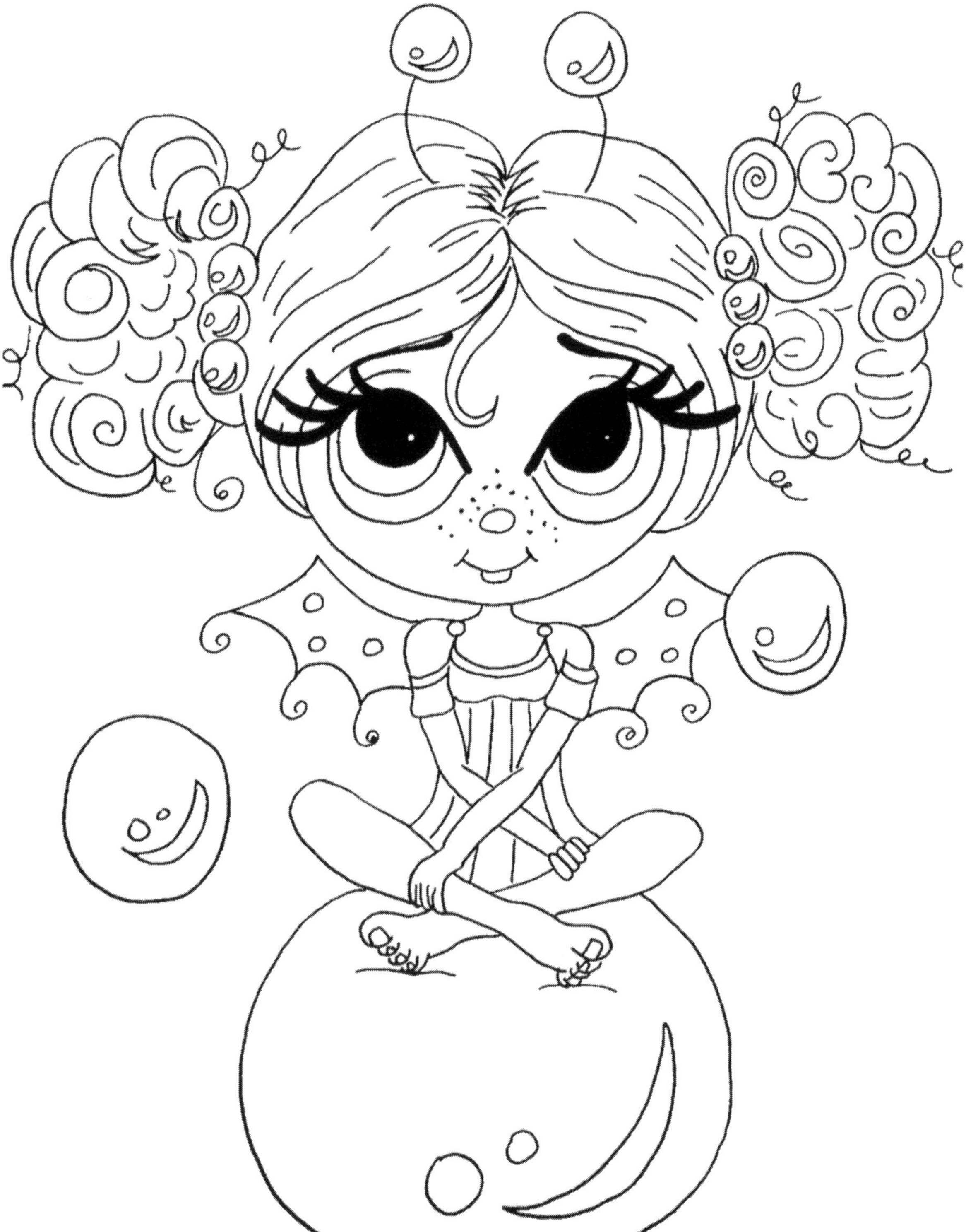

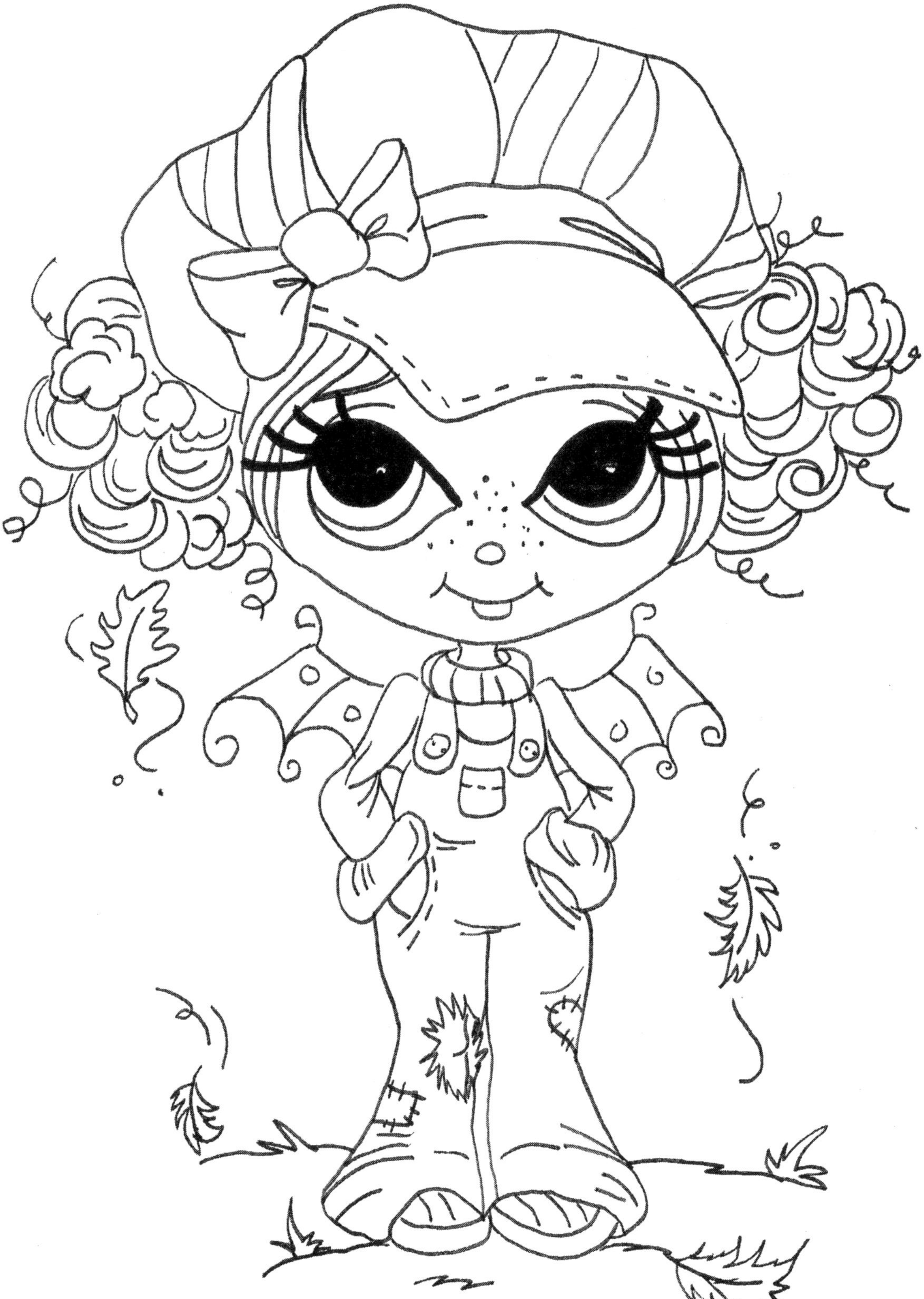

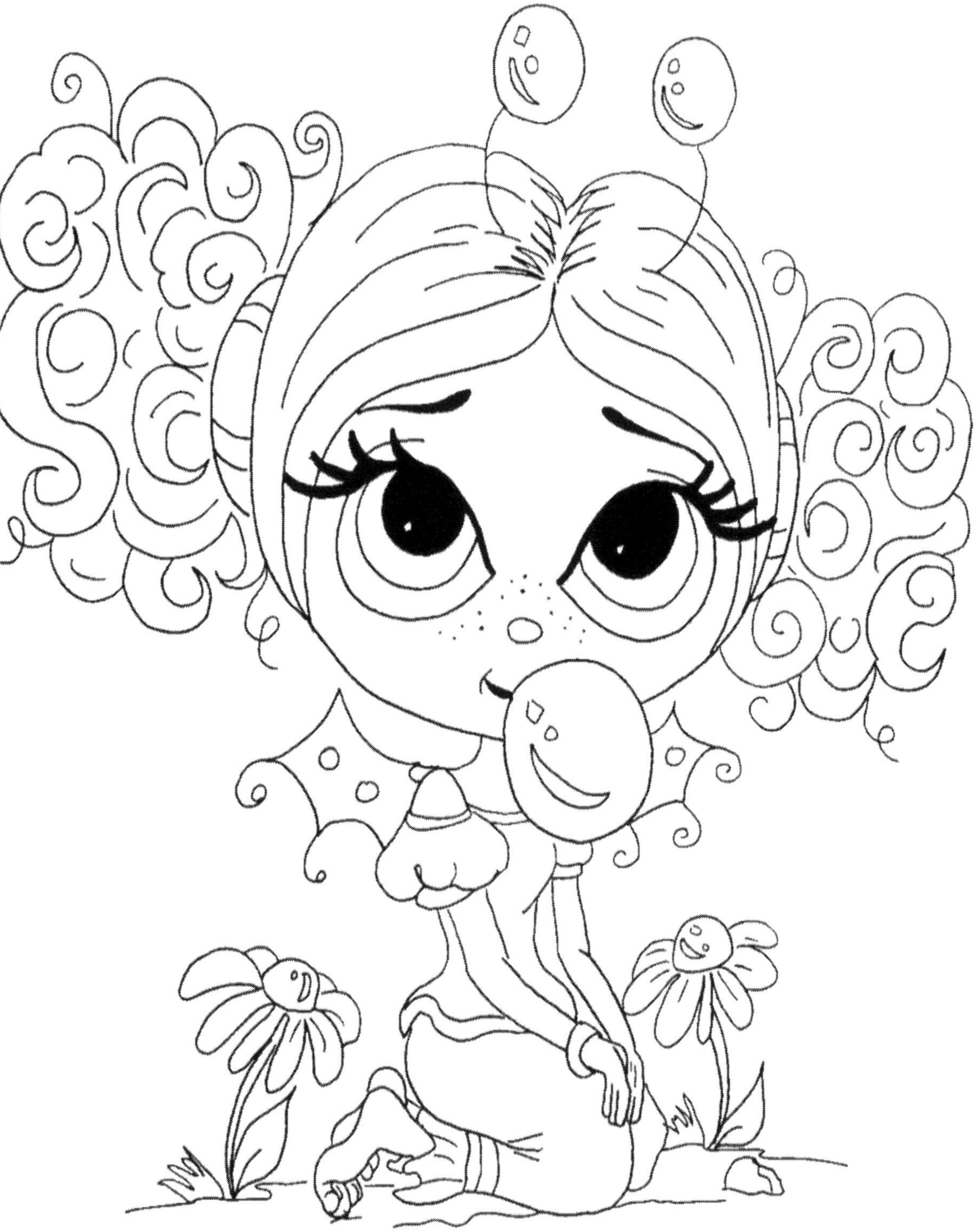

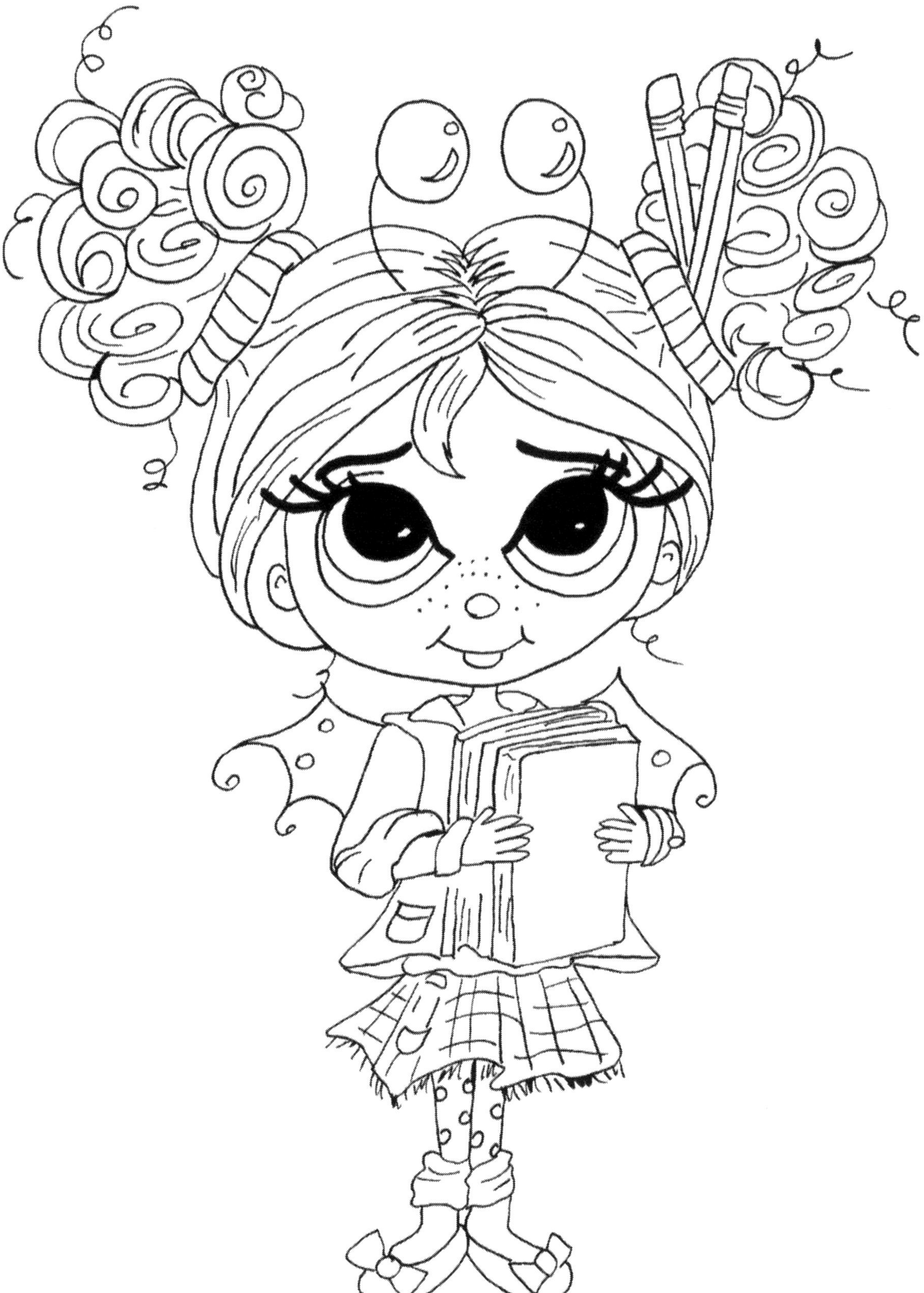

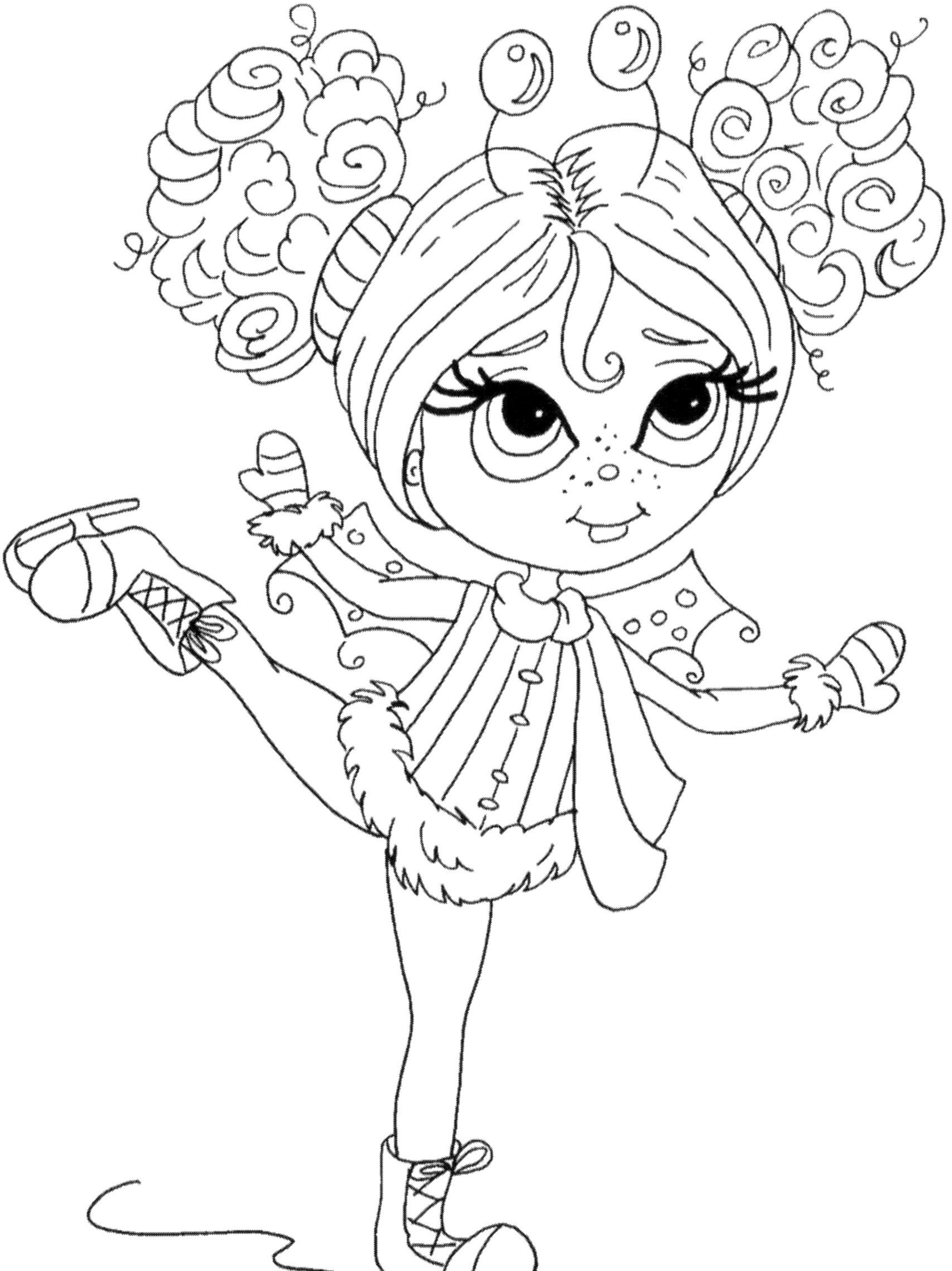

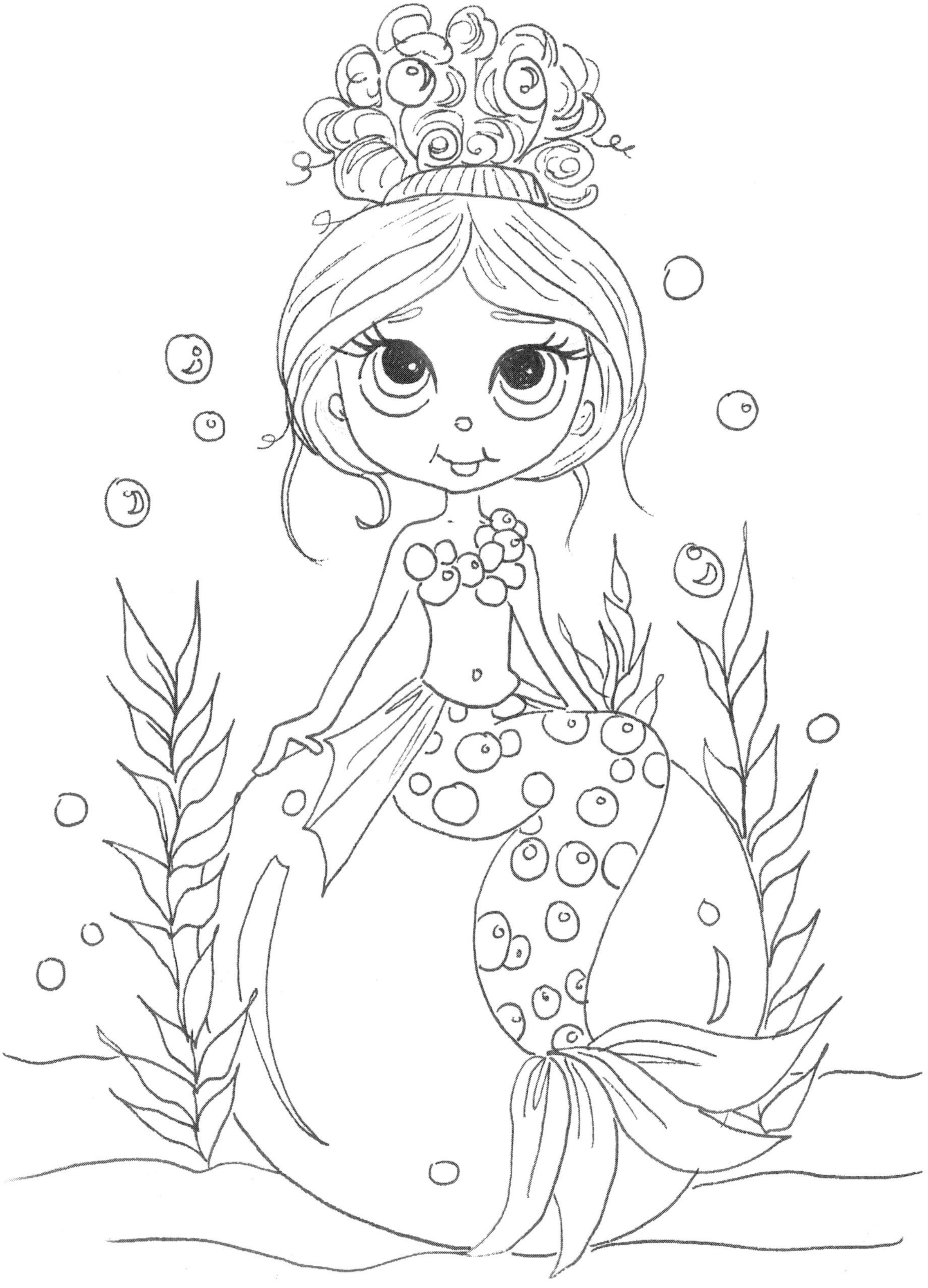

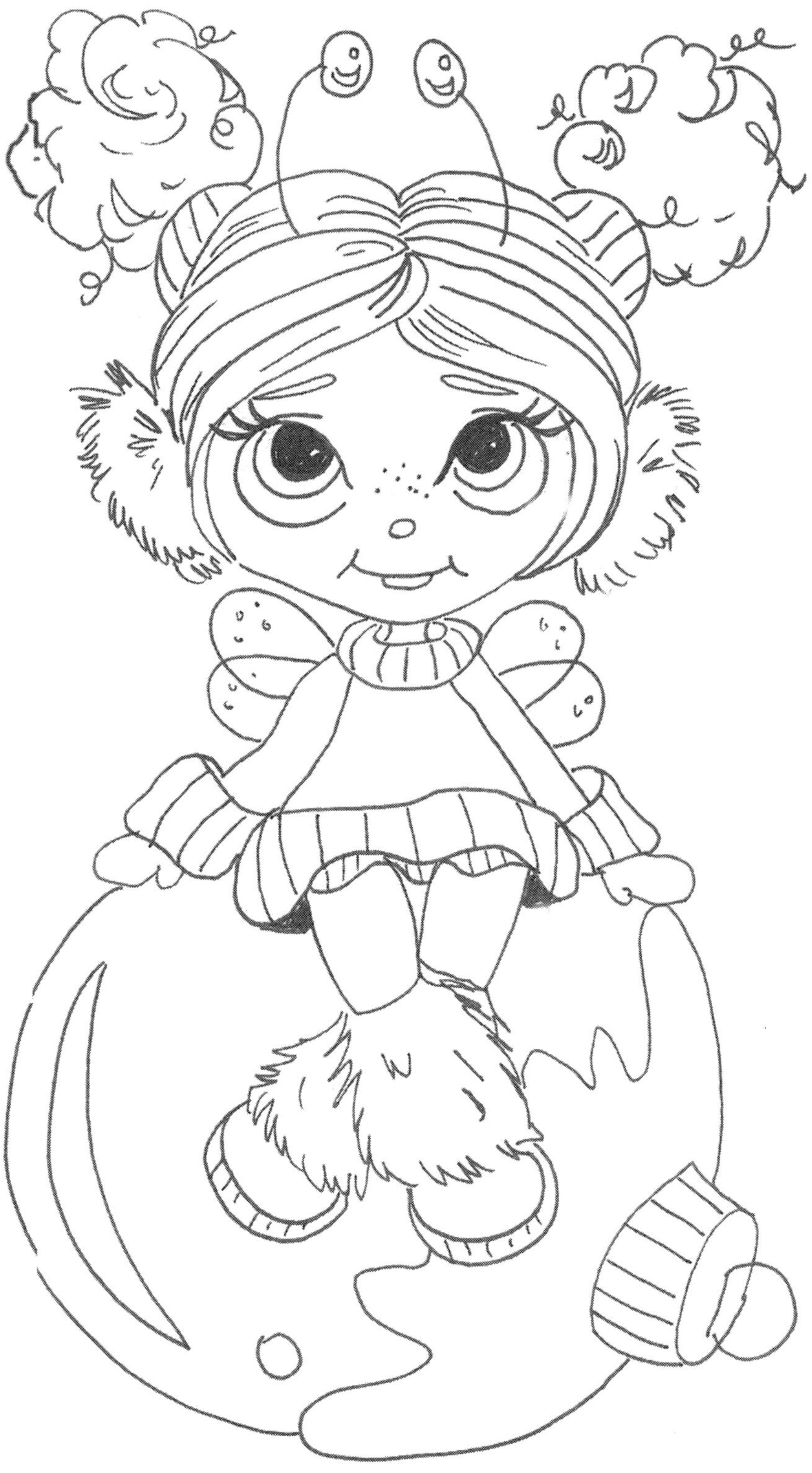

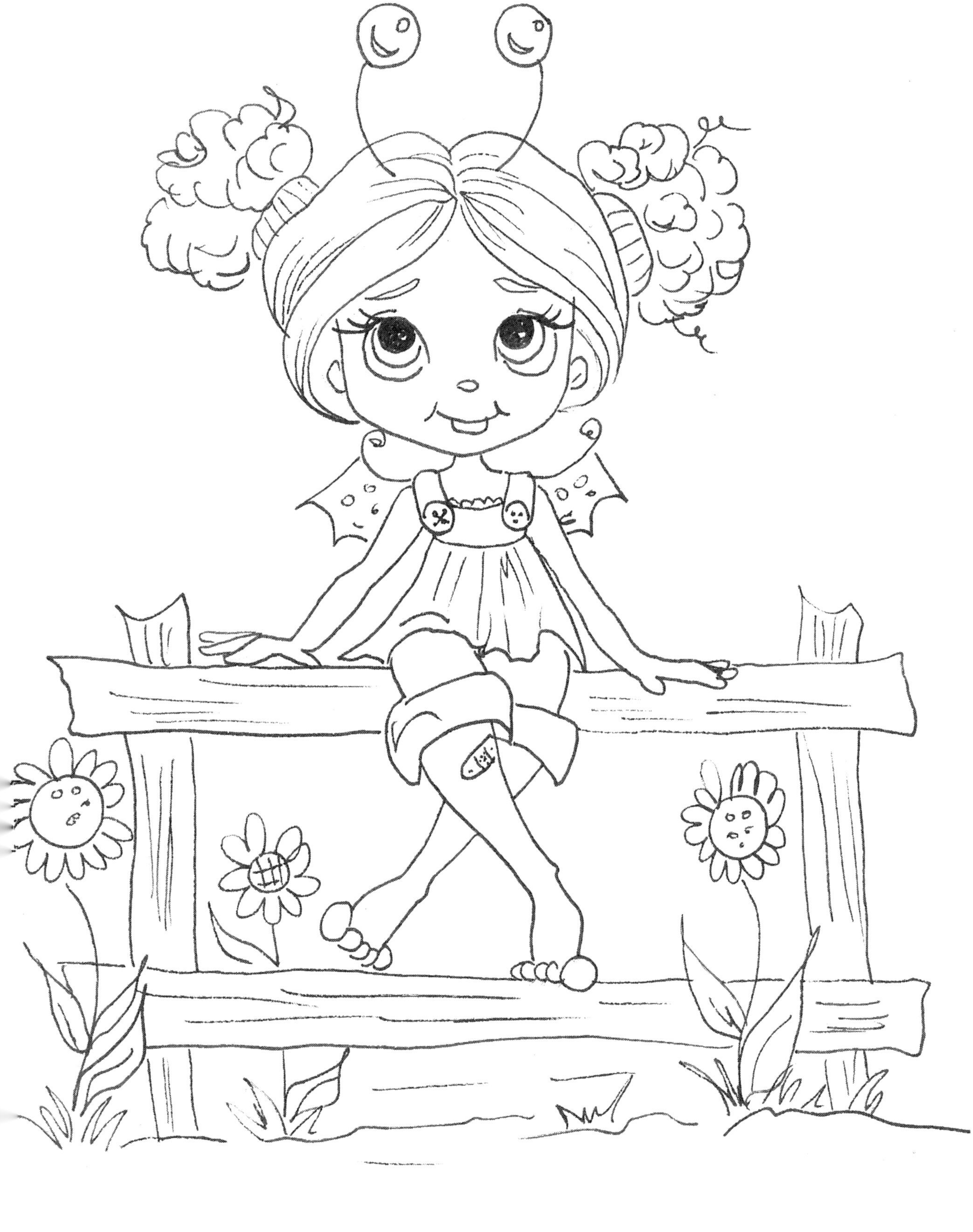

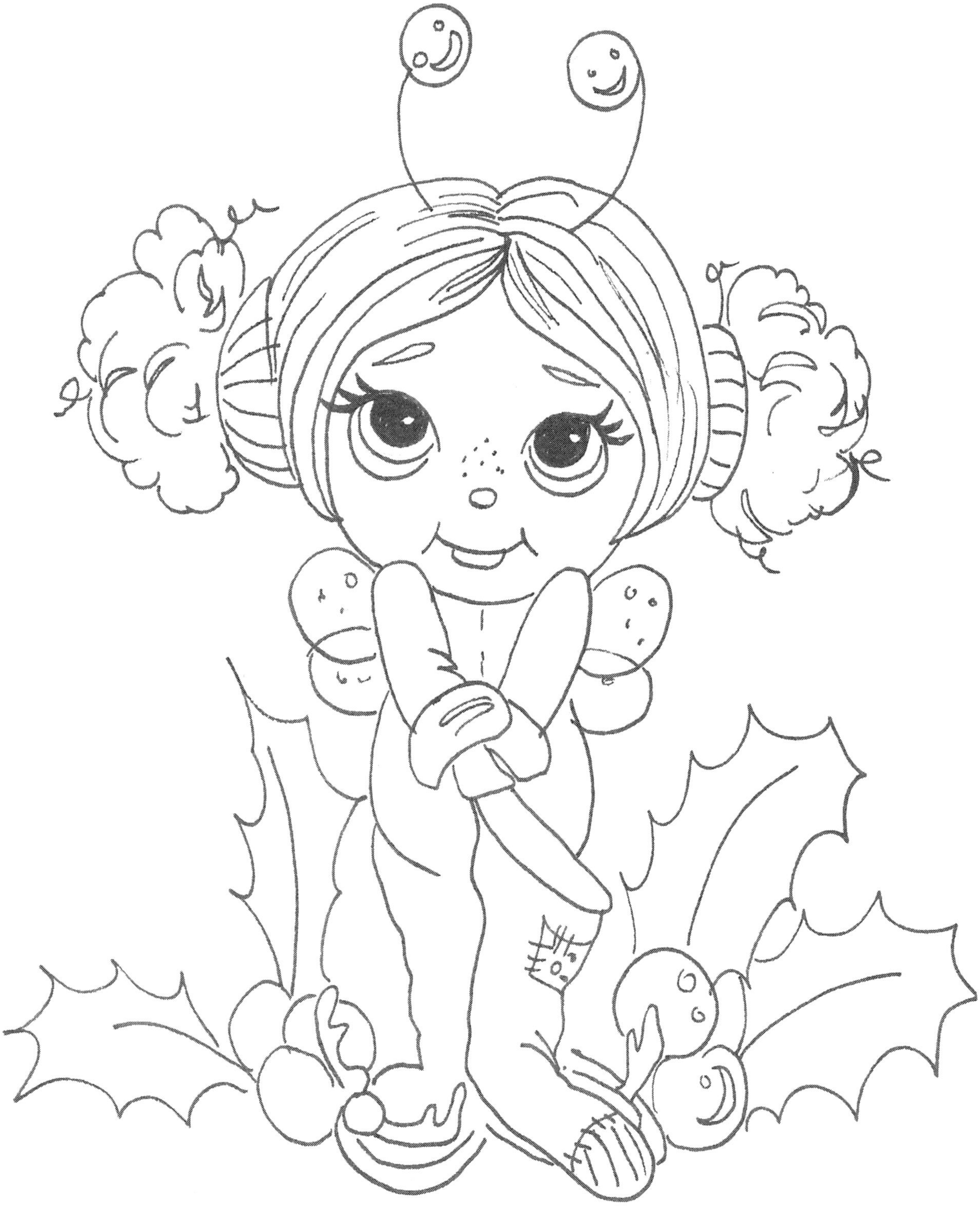

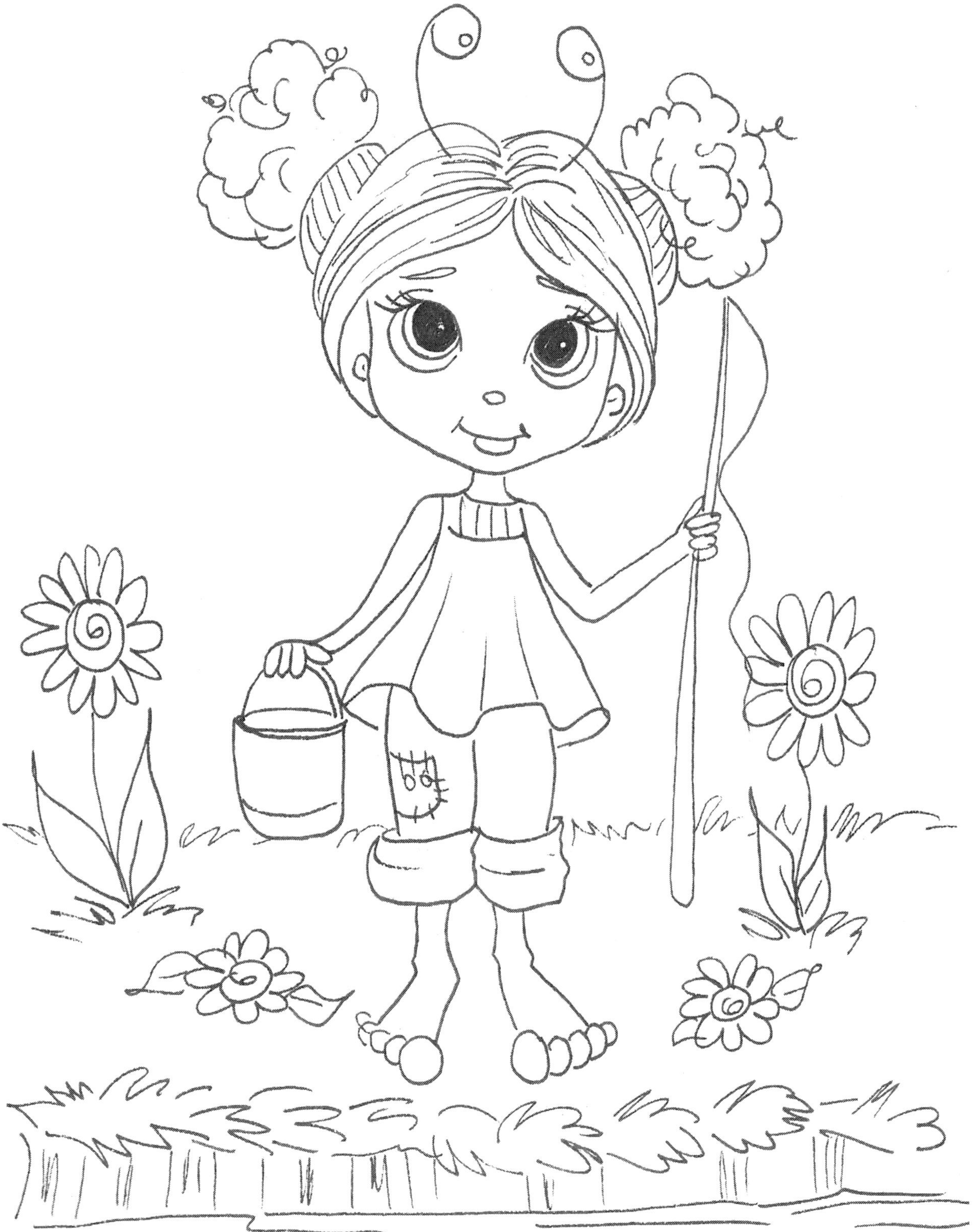

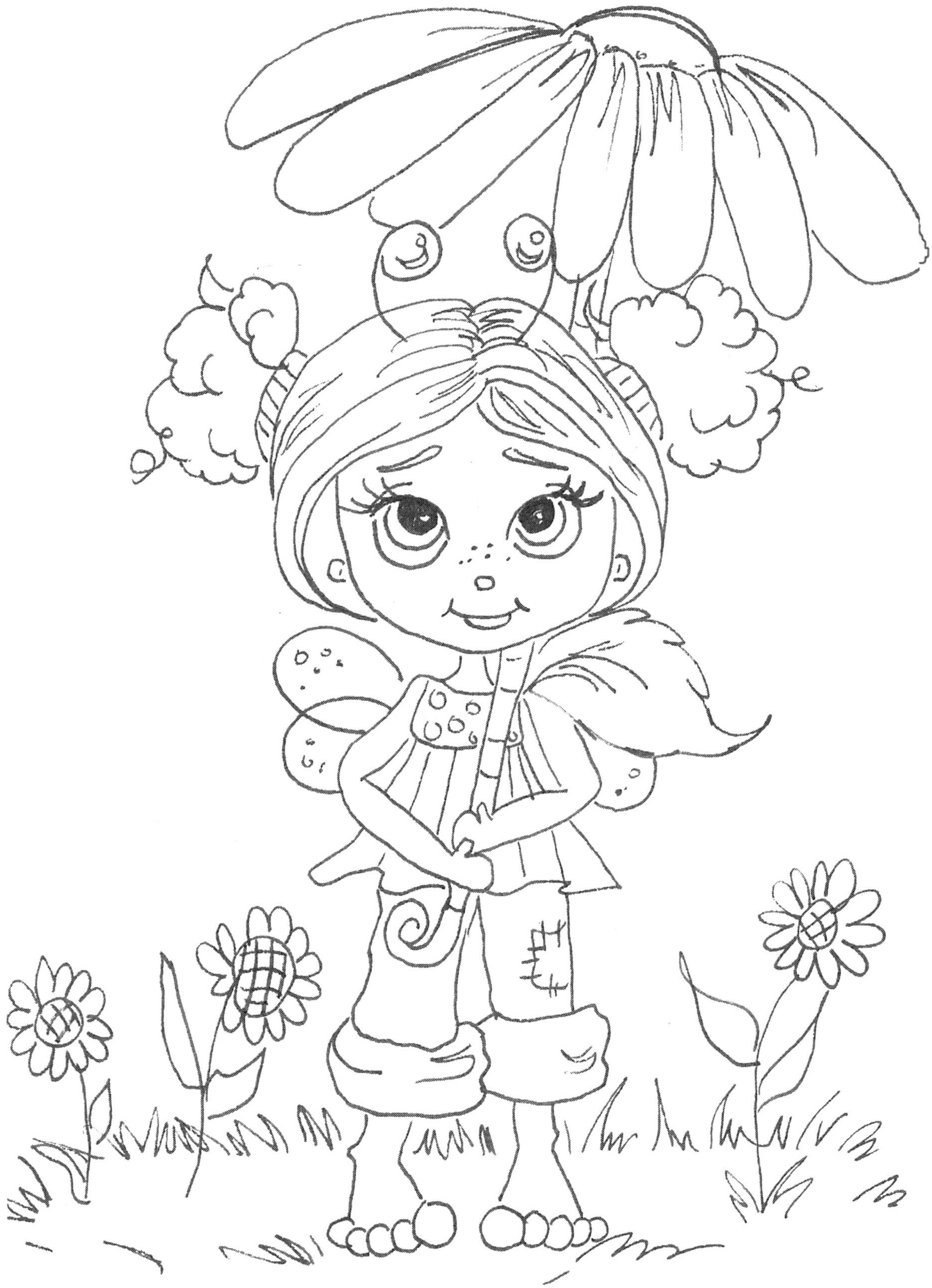

86022456R00031

Made in the USA
Lexington, KY
07 April 2018